101

QUOTES

to

IMPROVE YOUR

MINDSET, MOTIVATION & PERFORMANCE

ALLISTAIR McCAW

101 Quotes to Improve your Mindset, Motivation & Performance

First Edition – January 2025

Published by Allistair McCaw

Allistair McCaw
M

ISBN: 979-8-9922758-1-0
Library of Congress Cataloging-in-Publication Data

Library of Congress Case
McCaw, Allistair
101 Quotes to Improve your Mindset, Motivation
& Performance
Case Number: 1-14614752542 January 2025

Category: Motivation, Mindset, Self-Improvement, Performance

Author: Allistair McCaw

Format & Cover Design: EliJah Sr. & Jahshua Blyden | www.EliTheBookGuy.com

Printed in the USA by Book Bindery: A&A Printing & Publishing | www.PrintShopCentral.com

DISCLAIMER

INTRODUCTION

Having written several books on mindset, leadership and self-development over the past few years, the majority feedback from my readers is that they love the quotes. They find them inspiring, simple and impactful.

That's why I decided to compile 101 of the most downloaded and shared quotes from these books, as well as from my Instagram feed.

@bechampionminded

Allistair McCaw
M

MINDSET

When you upgrade
your mindset,
you upgrade your life.

#1

Switching your mindset from "I think I can" to "I'm going to make this happen" is a real game changer.

#2

Before you can win,
you must believe you
are a winner.
Winners think,
look, act, and behave
like winners.
They focus on the
daily process of
doing what needs
to be done to become
a winner.

#3

You can't expect to be at your best every day. However, no matter how you feel, always show up and give your best effort.

#4

Developing a stronger mindset is a skill that requires practice. Much the same as building a stronger body, you must put in the time and reps.

#5

Your biggest competition will always be yourself. Don't worry about what everyone else is doing. Just focus on becoming the best version of yourself.

#6

A winning mentality takes ownership.
A winning mentality doesn't accept average.
A winning mentality doesn't complain, make excuses or cast blame.

#7

A cool head wins a hot game. Being in control of your emotions when things become challenging is how you win games.

#8

Being mentally tough is keeping a positive mindset and composure when things become difficult and challenging.

#9

A positive mindset won't always guarantee you win. But a negative one will guarantee you always lose.

#10

Discipline is not
about perfection.
Discipline is about
staying committed
and being consistent.

#11

Consistency is key.
No results?
Keep working.
Poor results?
Keep working.
Great results?
Keep working.

#12

Self-talk is the most powerful form of communication.
It can either empower you or defeat you.

#13

Your level of growth comes down to how coachable and open you are to learning new things.

#14

The gap between where you want to be and where you are right now comes down to your habits, discipline and mindset.

#15

You can either suffer
the pain of discipline
or suffer the pain of
regret—the choice
is yours.

#16

Never let any person, any obstacle, any doubt, any fear, or negative voice keep you from becoming who you want to be. You get to decide that!

#17

Pressure is a
privilege.
Not everyone gets
to be out there
performing.

#18

Your self-belief is built through the words you say to yourself.
Winners talk to themselves like winners.

#19

Confidence is earned,
never given.
You earn it through
your preparation,
effort and mindset.

#20

The mindset of a champion is someone who has an unwavering belief in themselves and rises to the occasion when faced with adversity.

#21

You always win in the mind first. When you develop the right habits and mindset, you can overcome almost any obstacle or challenge.

#22

So many people try not to fail, whereas the great performers know that failure is part of the process and journey.

#23

A strong mindset is about learning from each experience, bouncing back from failure and focusing on long-term growth.

#24

The words you say to yourself matter. They affect everything – your mood, your energy, your body language, your self-belief and confidence.

#25

Confidence is like building a brick wall. When you recognize the small wins, you make daily, you add another brick to your confidence wall.

#26

Belief in yourself begins and ends with your mind.
You can talk yourself in to, or out of, almost anything.

#27

Cultivating a strong mindset takes practice, discipline, and a commitment to growth. It's an ongoing process.

#28

A winning mindset is a mix of resilience, focus, discipline and toughness.
These are the traits that drive champions to reach their goals, no matter the challenges.

#29

You become a
product of your most
dominant thoughts.
What you think,
you become.

#30

The hard is what makes it easy.
In other words, when you choose to stay disciplined now, life becomes easier later.

#31

You are not born a
winner.
You are not born a
loser.
You are born a
chooser.

#32

A bad attitude is like a flat tire.
If you don't change it, you'll never get anywhere.

#33

MOTIVATION

Success doesn't come from what you do occasionally.
Success comes from what you do consistently.

#34

To be in the top 1%, you need to be willing to do what the 99% won't.

#35

You can make excuses or you can make progress. Never both at the same time.

#36

Don't expect to feel inspired and motivated every day – even the best don't. Don't count on motivation, count on self-discipline.

#37

Talent might make you good, but it's your attitude and work-ethic that will make you great.

#38

A high work-ethic and good attitude puts you in places where good luck can find you.

#39

The goal is simple:
Aim to be better than
you were yesterday.

#40

One of the greatest determiners of success comes from having a purpose and hunger to succeed.

#41

Be grateful if you have someone in your life who pushes you to be better every day. Thank that person because not everyone gets to have that.

#42

Results happen over time, not overnight. Aim to stay consistent, work your hardest and keep believing in yourself.

#43

Excuses make today easy, but tomorrow hard. Discipline makes today hard, but tomorrow easy.

#44

Celebrate any progress, no matter how small. Don't wait for perfection. Recognizing your efforts each day helps build your confidence and motivation.

#45

Consistency is what transforms average into excellence.

#46

It's futile comparing
your progress
to others.
Everyone has their
own path.
Stay focused on yours
and trust the process.

#47

Remember that…
Hard work is a choice
Attitude is a choice
Discipline is a choice
Doing extra is
a choice

#48

A champion will always do more than what's been asked of them.

#49

A comfort zone is
a no progress zone.

#50

Every morning you get two choices: Continue sleeping with your dreams or wake up and chase them.

#51

Consistency wins.
It's not what you do
once in a while that
matters, it's what you
do every day.

#52

When someone tells
you it can't be done,
it's a reflection
of their limits,
not yours.

#53

You'd be surprised
who's watching your
journey and is
inspired by it.
Keep going.

#54

The only limits you
have are the ones you
place upon yourself.
Let go of limiting
beliefs and push
yourself to become
more.

#55

In the end, the number one underlying reason why the 5% succeed, be it in sports, business, or any other field for that matter, is because of this: They are willing to do more than what's been asked.

#56

The people who eventually succeed are the ones who have failed… a lot. They know that success involves learning from the many failures and lessons along the way.

#57

You become unstoppable when you work on things people can't take away from you. Things like your character, habits, mindset, and attitude.

#58

It's not about how
bad you want it.
It's about how hard
you're willing to
work for it.

#59

There will be times you feel you aren't making any progress – that's normal.
Just keep putting in the work and believe it's going to happen.

#60

A champion is not someone who wins all the time.
A champion is someone who gives everything they've got to win.

#61

To be successful at anything, you don't need to be more talented than others. You simply must be what most people aren't: **Consistent**.

#62

It's not luck.
It's called hard work,
early mornings,
late nights and
sacrificing short term
gratification for long
term gains.

#63

There are no limits to what you can achieve. The only limits that exist are the ones in your mind.

#64

Consistency is harder when no one is supporting or clapping for you. You must clap for yourself during those times. Always be your biggest fan.

#65

You will have good days, bad days, overwhelming days, tired days, awesome days, I can't go days – and everyday you'll keep showing up.

This is the mindset of a champion.

#66

Never let perfection
get in the way of
becoming your best.
Learn to find joy
in the process of
becoming and
be content in doing
your best.

#67

I've never met a lazy person who achieved excellence.
Excellence requires getting out of your comfort zone and doing the things others don't have the discipline to do.

#68

PERFORMANCE

How you think affects how you perform.

Negative input = negative output.

Positive input = positive output.

#69

To perform at your peak, you need to prepare like a champion, think like a champion, behave like a champion and perform like a champion.

#70

You can't practice soft and expect to play hard.
How you compete is a direct reflection of how you train and prepare.

#71

High performers are
the best at finding
solutions to problems
faster.
Poor performers
spend their energy
complaining about
the problem and
looking for who
to blame.

#72

The highest performers in their fields are continuous learners and stay coachable.
No matter what heights they reach, they just keep wanting to get better.

#73

A high-performance mindset is about bringing your best attitude, giving your best effort, and embracing high pressure moments.

#74

The best performers
are committed to
excellence.
They have built
consistent habits and
routines that lead to
success.

#75

High performance is all about the ability to overcome adversity quickly, stay focused on the goal, and keep putting in maximum effort.

#76

The difference between winning and losing can be a millimeter or a millisecond.
Never underestimate the importance of the small details.

#77

High performers have a high level of self-awareness. They know their strengths and weaknesses. They also reflect on how their attitude and behaviors affect their performances.

#78

The more you are willing to fail and learn, the closer you get to success. Failure is not the opposite of success; it's a part of it.

#79

You might not be the most talented, but there is zero excuse not to be the hardest worker.

#80

Attention to detail is key. If you can't do the little things right, you will never do the big things right.

#81

High performance is about controlling the controllables.
The best performers don't waste their energy worrying about the things they have no control over.

#82

To perform at your peak, you need to make sure you are surrounding yourself with people who are on the same mission as you.

#83

Progress doesn't come without discomfort.
The more uncomfortable you are willing to get, the more progress you will make.

#84

Improving your performances is about learning to recognize and celebrate your small daily wins. This is how you build confidence and self-belief.

#85

The best performers are always self-assessing their performances.
Win or lose, they have a deep desire to understand how and why they achieved that result.

#86

High performers know that excellence doesn't come from doing easy things. It comes from a willingness to do the uncomfortable and hard stuff.

#87

The best performers don't allow distractions to interfere when they perform. Through the many hours of practice, they have trained their minds to be locked in and focused.

#88

Hard work and persistence pay off.

Maybe not today, maybe not tomorrow.

But eventually it pays off.

#89

Excellence isn't about the outcome.

Excellence is about the effort you give.

You can't control the outcomes, but you can control the effort you give.

#90

High performers
crave feedback.
They don't just wait
for it; they ask for it.
They aren't afraid to
be told the truth.

#91

A large part of being able to perform at a high level comes down to the environment and people you choose.

The right ones will propel you. The wrong ones will deplete you.

#92

No one can make you better. You can have the world's best coaches and mentors advising you,
but in the end,
it's all on you.

#93

Remember that when you drive high standards, not everyone will agree or align with them. But then again, not everyone drives excellence.

#94

Don't take shortcuts or cut corners. When you skip the small details, you not only cheat yourself, you sell yourself short of success.

#95

Achieving high performance all starts in the mind. You must first see it in your mind before you can achieve it.

See it. Believe it. Achieve it.

#96

Being a high
performer isn't about
being talented
or gifted.
Being a high
performer is about
effort, discipline
and consistency.

#97

To accelerate your progress in whatever field you are endeavoring, aim to surround yourself with people who have already achieved what you wish to achieve.

#98

You don't need to tell others how invested you are. Your level of effort will show that.

#99

High performance is about sticking to the process, believing in the process, and not being afraid to pivot or adjust direction when required.

#100

High performers
are brilliant at
these 3 things:

1. Paying attention
to the small details

2. The monotony
of repetition

3. Problem solving

#101

.

SHARE
Your Favorite Quote
on Allistair's Instagram

@bechampionminded

Allistair McCaw

INSPIRED BY

The 101 Quotes in this book have been taken from some of Allistair's best works:

www.ingramcontent.com/pod-product-compliance
Lightning Source LLC
Chambersburg PA
CBHW061657120626
46550CB00003B/980